A New Home For Harley

BRENDA HOIT RIFFE

Fulton Books, Inc.
Meadville, PA

Published by Fulton Books 2021

ISBN 978-1-63710-545-0 (paperback)
ISBN 978-1-63710-546-7 (digital)

Printed in the United States of America

To Madison and Nicholas.

I love you to the moon and back…and more.

It was cold outside. I was drawing circles on the window above me. I could see my breath on the window as Jax stretched out his legs beside me, kicking me in his sleep.

It seemed like a long time since my mom left. It was in the daylight, but now it is dark. I can only see shadows under the street lamps. My tummy begins to growl again.

I was awakened by voices outside my window.

"Hey, sweetie," a lady said. "Can you unlock the window?"

Was she talking to me? There was a policeman with her. I could barely see him through the blue lights and my foggy windows, but I knew he was a policeman. He looked just like the guy who knocked on our door at home one time. He was wearing the same kind of uniform, and his badge reflected when the light from his flashlight hit it.

"Let's go get you something to eat and get you warm. Sweetie, would you unlock the door for me?" I slowly reached out and unlocked the door. I could do it all by myself. Unlike my little brother, I could do lots of things by myself. I was going to be five years old in only eight more months. My hands were so cold. It was hard for me, but I did it.

The lady slowly opened the door and took me up in her arms. She threw a blanket around us as we walked toward the police car.

"What is your name? You are such a good-looking little boy!"

"Harley," I whispered. "My brother's name is Jackson."

The policeman threw a blanket around my little brother and put us in the back seat with the lady. I was shivering. I wasn't cold anymore, but I was still shivering.

It seemed like a long ride because I fell asleep. The police car came to a stop outside a little house. I could see a man and woman looking out the window, and they opened the door for us.

"I want to go to my house," I told the lady. "I want *my* mommy." My brother woke up and started to cry.

The policeman handed him to the man who started patting him and bouncing him up and down. He took him into the kitchen. The lady in the house came out and wrapped one of her blankets around me. It smelled just like it came out of the dryer.

"It's okay, Harley," she said. "My name is Sarah, and my husband's name is Kevin. We are going to take care of you for a while until we can find your mommy." She handed me a stuffed bear wearing a big bow around its neck. It still had the tags on it, and she tucked it under my blanket with me.

We walked into the kitchen where Jackson was eating a banana on Kevin's lap.

"I'm not hungry."

"Okay," Sarah said. "How about just a cup of soup? It will warm you up, and I made it just for you."

"I hate soup," I said. I took the mug from her hand and took a drink. "I don't like soup, and I *hate* tomato soup!"

I took another drink, then another. I didn't tell anyone that night, not anyone. But that was the best cup of soup I had ever eaten.

It felt like I was asleep for two whole days. When I woke up, Jackson was in a little bed beside mine. He slid off on his belly, and he took off running as soon as his feet hit the floor. I looked around the room. I could see so many toys and things around me. I didn't know what a lot of them even were, and I'm almost five! I crawled out of my bed and stared in awe at the toys on the shelf. I tried to pick up a big green dinosaur, but it was so big I needed both of my hands. It was so cool and felt like a real dinosaur. Then it happened. It roared. It scared me, and I dropped it. Its head came off, so I picked it up and threw it.

I picked up the car next to it and threw it too. I threw all the toys on the shelf. I even picked up that stuffed bear Sarah gave me last night, and I threw that too! I threw that bear the hardest and farthest that I could.

Sarah came into the room. She saw the mess of thrown toys, and she saw my tears rolling down my face. She didn't yell at me or hit me. She bent down near me and put her arm around me.

"It's going to be okay, Harley. It's okay to feel angry, and it's okay to be sad and scared," she said.

She picked me up like I was Jackson, and she rocked me in her arms. I'm too old to be rocked like that, I thought, but I'm going to let her. Just this one time.

Days and nights went by. Sarah and Kevin enrolled me in preschool. Jax can't go because he's too little—you have to be old like me. Sarah said I would make lots of friends there.

My first day was a little scary. I had to sit real still on the carpet while Miss Rachel read us a story. We got to stand up and get our wiggles out. I didn't even know I had those things! She even had puppets that talked to us about our feelings and how to take deep breaths instead of throwing our toys. Miss Rachel told me I was just the little boy she needed to make her class complete. She made a special sticker chart just for me. And for lunch, we had warm tomato soup.

I think I'm going to like this place.

21

When I got home, Sarah and Kevin made me a snack and told me they wanted to talk to me. "Your mom did the very best she could trying to take care of you and Jackson," Sarah explained. "She is not able to take you back, and Kevin and I would like to be your mom and dad." Tears were coming out of my eyes so fast I couldn't stop them. I missed my mom every single day, but it was getting easier. Sarah picked me up and wiped away my tears. "Will you think about it?" she asked.

I nodded slowly.

That night, Sarah made so many bubbles in my and Jax's bath! We couldn't pop them fast enough! Jax's giggles echoed in the bathtub. I liked watching him laugh. It made me laugh too.

Sarah tucked my bear next to me and tickled me when she covered me up in bed. She kissed my forehead. "I love you, my little prince," she said.

"I love you, Momma," I whispered. Sarah stopped and looked at me with tears in her eyes. "My heart is big enough for a new family. After all, I'm almost five."

About the Illustrator

Nathan West was born and raised in West Virginia and now resides in Pittsburgh, Pennsylvania. He works both as a freelance graphic designer and a manager of a residential facility for children and teens with behavioral problems that are also Deaf.

Many of the character depictions in the book are real people that work in the same facility as Nathan to positively impact children's and teen's lives. Nathan also explained he uses the orange/yellow color in the illustrations as a metaphor for light, goodness, and hope. Harley himself is always depicted in orange/yellow, and as things improve for Harley throughout the book, more orange/yellow is added into the illustrations. The illustrations also begin with colors that are very muted to emphasize the situation itself is dark, and as the book progresses, colors become more saturated, bright, and warm. If you would like to contact Nathan or see more of his work visit: westgraphicdesign.com.

About the Author

Brenda H. Riffe lives in Charleston, West Virginia, where she works as a preschool education manager. She lives with her Yorkie Chewy and has two wonderful children, whom are the love of her life, Madison and Nicholas.

Brenda holds a master's degree in preschool special needs birth to five and severe and profound education from West Virginia University and received her leadership from Salem University.

She has worked with preschool and special needs population for over thirty years and was moved to write *A New Home for Harley* after seeing the effects of trauma on young children in the state of West Virginia. She hopes this book will provide a source of hope, healing, and happy endings for all kids.

Lightning Source UK Ltd.
Milton Keynes UK
UKHW020241240322
400477UK00029B/500

9 781637 105450